SO-AVG-917

Louis Armstrong

History Maker Bios

Judith Pinkerton Josephson

LERNER PUBLICATIONS COMPANY • MINNEAPOLIS

To Ron, Kirsten, and Erika, for their love and support

For their insightful suggestions and help, thanks to Edith, Donna, Karen, Connie, Jodie, Suzan, and Marie. For his attention to detail and appreciation of Louis Armstrong, thanks to my editor, Jeffrey Zuehlke.

Illustrations by Tad Butler.

Text copyright © 2008 by Judith Pinkerton Josephson
Illustrations copyright © 2008 by Lerner Publications Company

All rights reserved. International copyright secured. No part of this book may be reproduced, stored in a retrieval system, or transmitted in any form or by any means—electronic, mechanical, photocopying, recording, or otherwise—without the prior written permission of Lerner Publishing Group, Inc., except for the inclusion of brief quotations in an acknowledged review.

Lerner Publications Company
A division of Lerner Publishing Group, Inc.
241 First Avenue North
Minneapolis, MN 55401 U.S.A.

Website address: http://www.lernerbooks.com

Library of Congress Cataloging-in-Publication Data

Josephson, Judith Pinkerton.
  Louis Armstrong / by Judith P. Josephson.
    p.   cm. — (History maker bios)
  Includes bibliographical references (p.   ) and index.
  ISBN-13: 978–0–8225–7169–8 (lib. bdg. : alk. paper)
    1. Armstrong, Louis, 1901–1971—Juvenile literature. 2. Jazz musicians—United States—Biography—Juvenile literature. 3. African American jazz musicians—Biography—Juvenile literature. I. Title.
  ML3930.A75J67 2008
  781.65092—dc22 [B]   2007014744

Manufactured in the United States of America
1 2 3 4 5 6 – JR – 13 12 11 10 09 08

TABLE OF CONTENTS

INTRODUCTION

Among the best-loved musical sounds of the 1900s were the sweet, jazzy notes that poured from Louis Armstrong's horn. Just as famous was Louis's rough, gravelly voice. This beloved entertainer played with boundless energy for crowds all over the world.

Because of his big, broad smile, the King of Jazz had many nicknames. Some people called him Dippermouth or Gatemouth. But to most fans, he was simply Satchmo. As Ambassador Satch, Louis spread goodwill and a love for jazz wherever he went.

This is his story.

1 "COAL CART BLUES"

People say jazz music began in New Orleans, Louisiana. Some even claim to know the exact date—August 4, 1901. That was the day Louis Armstrong was born.

Louis grew up in a poor African American neighborhood in New Orleans. His father had left the family when Louis was just a boy. Louis lived with his younger sister, Beatrice, and his mother, Mayann. Everybody respected his mother. Louis always said she had a beautiful soul.

Mayann had to work hard to make sure her children had a place to live and food to eat. Sometimes she could only afford biscuits and gravy or day-old bread. To help out, Louis did small jobs and sang on street corners for money.

Louis grew up in a neighborhood called Storyville (RIGHT). The houses there were small and did not have backyards.

Mayann taught Louis and Beatrice to use good common sense. Always respect others, Mayann told her children. The family prayed at meals and before bed. Louis kept this habit his whole life.

In 1908, two good things happened to Louis. He entered a boys' school where he learned to read and write. He also met the Karnofskys, a Jewish family from Russia. When he wasn't in school, Louis worked for the Karnofskys. He and their oldest son drove a wagon house to house, selling coal.

This pendant is a Star of David, a symbol of the Jewish faith. Throughout his life, Louis wore such a pendant in honor of the Karnofsky family.

This is Louis's first horn. It is a brass cornet.

After the boys finished their work, Mrs. Karnofsky often fixed Louis a plate of food. He loved her cooking, especially a thin, crisp bread called matzo. She taught him a Russian lullaby and other songs. From her, he learned to sing from his heart.

Passing a store window one day, Louis spotted a battered brass horn. The Karnofskys lent him five dollars to buy it. Louis had his first instrument! He struggled to make rough, wobbly sounds with the cornet. But he longed to take lessons. He knew he had music in his soul.

When Louis was eleven, he dropped out of school. He began hanging around with tough kids and getting into trouble. On New Year's Day, 1913, he fired a pistol into the air. Louis was arrested and sent to a home for troubled black boys.

Louis cried and cried. The Colored Waif's Home felt like a jail to him. But he soon discovered that the home had a music teacher, Peter Davis. With Mr. Davis, Louis studied the tambourine, snare drum, alto horn, bugle, and cornet. "I was in seventh heaven," said Louis.

At the Colored Waif's Home, Louis (CIRCLED) learned to play different instruments in the brass band.

Joe "King" Oliver (BACK, THIRD FROM LEFT) played the cornet and directed the band during performances.

Louis Armstrong left the boys' home when he was twelve. His school days ended. But Louis knew what he wanted to do with his life—make music. Joe "King" Oliver was one of New Orleans's best bandleaders and trumpet players. Joe befriended Louis, giving him music lessons and paying him to do odd jobs.

In time, when bands needed an extra horn player, they came looking for "little Louis." Some nights, all he earned was fifteen cents. But Louis loved playing for people.

By age seventeen, Louis and his cornet were in demand. He played in dance halls, at parades, and at funerals. In New Orleans, funerals weren't sad events. They celebrated a person's life. Mourners believed music helped send the dead person's soul to heaven.

Black musicians were creating an exciting new kind of music in New Orleans—jazz. It danced with bright, lively melodies and bouncy rhythms. During solos, musicians often made up the music as they went along. This is called improvising.

HONKY-TONKS AND NEW ORLEANS JAZZ

Jazz music began in New Orleans's poor black neighborhoods. At night, people went to places called honky-tonks. At nightclubs like Butcher Hill Hall, folks listened to music and danced. Louis and other young kids often gathered outside. Feet tapping, they danced on the sidewalk to the jazz music they heard from inside.

Louis had his picture taken with his mother, Mayann (CENTER), and his sister, Beatrice (RIGHT), in 1918.

"Music was all around you," said Louis. "Music kept you rolling." Some nights, Louis blew his cornet so long and hard that his lip split open and bled.

In 1919, Louis began a wonderful new job. Bandleader Fate Marable hired him to play in his riverboat band. In those days, people often took cruises on the river. They danced and listened to live music as the riverboats steamed up and down the Mississippi River.

For three summers, Louis amazed listeners with his exciting playing. One musician said Louis's horn sounded "hot, sweet, and pure."

Meanwhile, jazz was spreading around the country. Louis's friend Joe Oliver had moved to Chicago, Illinois. His Creole Jazz Band was a big hit there. In the summer of 1922, Joe asked Louis to come to Chicago and join his band.

On a hot August day, Mayann Armstrong packed her son a trout sandwich. She insisted that he wear long underwear under his clothes. She worried he would get cold on the train. Then twenty-one-year-old Louis headed north to Chicago.

2 "HEEBIE JEEBIES"

Louis had never seen a city as big and busy as Chicago. He gawked at the tall buildings and the rushing crowds. Luckily, he wouldn't be on his own. The Olivers let him stay with them until he got settled. Louis liked to type letters. So right away, he bought a typewriter so he could write letters to family and friends back home.

When he first heard King Oliver's Creole Jazz Band, Louis worried. Was he good enough to join them? But with each passing day, his confidence grew. On cornet duets, Joe and Louis made perfect harmony. Soon, people in Chicago were talking about Louis's unique horn style and strong rhythm.

In 1923, he made his first recording with the band as a soloist. Listeners around the country could buy these records and hear Louis play.

Louis (KNEELING, PLAYING SLIDE TRUMPET) poses with King Oliver's Creole Jazz Band. Lil Hardin sits at the piano.

Louis's joyful smile was nearly as popular as his trumpet playing.

Louis's life was changing fast. He fell in love with the band's piano player, Lil Hardin. She was smart, pretty, and college educated. In February 1924, they married.

Meanwhile, Louis's playing earned more and more attention. Later that year, he got a message from one of the country's top African American bandleaders. Fletcher Henderson asked Louis to join his band in New York City. Louis wasn't sure. He was happy in Joe Oliver's band. Why should he leave? But Lil talked her husband into accepting the offer. She stayed behind to work in Chicago.

Louis (BACK, THIRD FROM LEFT) joined the Fletcher Henderson Orchestra in 1924. Henderson is seated at the piano.

Jazz was new, and Louis Armstrong was a new kind of performer. At first, other New York musicians thought he was just a backward country boy. They changed their minds when they heard his cornet. His powerful playing bounced off the walls of even the largest rooms. Up on stage, he smiled as wide as a piano keyboard. His brown eyes sparkled.

Soon, crowds hurried to Harlem, the black neighborhood of New York City. They wanted to hear Louis. The band also played in nightclubs all over New England. No black band had ever done that before.

While in New York, Louis recorded forty songs. In those days, bands gathered in a studio to make records. The musicians set up and played in front of a big microphone. Louis's playing was so loud that he had to stand far behind the rest of the band. Otherwise, his cornet drowned out everyone else.

After fourteen months in New York, Louis went home to Chicago. He began playing trumpet as well as cornet. (Trumpets are like cornets. But trumpets have a louder tone and a wider range of notes.) Soon few other trumpeters could match Louis.

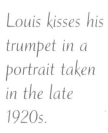

Louis kisses his trumpet in a portrait taken in the late 1920s.

Louis dazzled audiences. In return, their clapping and shouts gave him energy. During pauses in songs called breaks, the other musicians stopped playing. Louis would keep going, wowing the crowd with his solos. He could play high notes better than anyone else.

"I used to hit forty or fifty high C [notes], go wild, screaming on my horn," said Louis. "I was nuts." Sometimes he held high notes for ten seconds or longer. He could also make his trumpet talk with a jazzy "wah-wah-wah" sound.

Louis (LEFT) was always laughing and having fun. Here he jokes around with a friend before a show.

This playful poster advertises Louis's new song, "I'm a Ding Dong Daddy (from Dumas)." Fans could buy the record for seventy-five cents.

I'm a Ding Dong Daddy

It lures! ...you swing into its passionate beat of music and joyously sense the throb of its rhythm

«I'm A Ding Dong Daddy» (From DUMAS)

«I'm In The Market For You»
FOX TROTS - VOCAL REFRAINS

Louis Armstrong
and His Sebastian New Cotton Club
ORCHESTRA

75¢   75
★ ★ R A C E   OKeh   R E C O R D S
ELECTRIC
№. 41442   №. 41442
Okeh Phonograph Corporation, 1819 Broadway, New York, N. Y.

But Louis didn't just play music. He also made audiences laugh. Sometimes he dressed as a preacher in an old black coat and gave funny pretend sermons. He wrinkled his nose. He raised his eyebrows and rolled his eyes. Sweat streamed down his face. He mopped it up with a white handkerchief. Audiences loved every minute of his act.

In time, Armstrong formed his own band with Lil and three others. They called themselves the Hot Five.

Around 1926, Louis and the Hot Five recorded a song called "Heebie Jeebies." During the recording, Louis stopped following the written words and notes. Instead, he made up nonsense words, like "skid-dat-de-dat" or "ba-ba-bo-zet." The song became a big hit. And everyone loved Louis's made-up words. After that, "scat singing" became part of jazz.

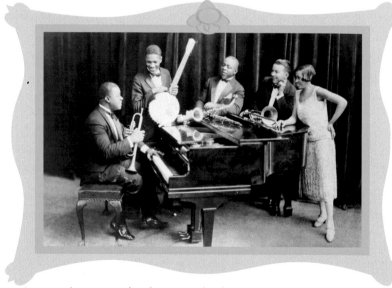

Louis (AT PIANO) chats with the Hot Five in Chicago. Lil (FAR RIGHT) played the piano in the band.

HOT FIVE AND HOT SEVEN

Jazz lovers say the recordings of Louis Armstrong and his Hot Five band are some of the best ever made. Later, the Hot Five became the Hot Seven, when two more players joined them. In three years, the band made sixty-five records. Songs had catchy titles, like "Gut Bucket Blues," "Muskrat Ramble," and "Potato Head Blues."

Over the years, Louis had often sent money home to his mother in New Orleans. When she became sick in 1927, Louis brought her to Chicago. Mayann died that summer. But before she passed away, she told him how proud she was of his success. When his mother's coffin was lowered into the ground, tears fell from Louis's eyes. What would he do without his dear mother? "I just couldn't stop crying," he said later.

3 "SLEEPYTIME DOWN SOUTH"

"A note's a note in any language," Louis Armstrong once said. "Jazz will give you beautiful ideas, make you feel good." By the age of twenty-eight, he was world famous. The king of Great Britain even gave Louis a special trumpet.

*In London,
England, Louis
tried on the latest
British fashions.
He wore a woolen
suit and cap with
multicolored
socks.*

Cheering crowds made Louis want to put on a good show. "People love me and my music and you know I love them," he said. "The minute I walk on the bandstand, they know they're going to get something good." In 1929, Louis Armstrong and his band worked again in New York City. They played every night at a well-known Harlem nightclub.

Louis thought a musician should have an original style. Practicing and practicing, he worked to form his own. He wove new melodies and rhythms into the songs he played. He could hit deep low notes. He rippled up the scale to screaming high notes. Once he played 250 high Cs in a row.

Louis's gruff voice was one of a kind. As he sang more, he made some phrases short and some long. His singing became as creative as his trumpet playing.

Louis sent out copies of this portrait. He sometimes labeled it "Louis Armstrong: World's Greatest Trumpeter."

Louis (LEFT) loved to have his picture taken, especially for silly photos. Here he and some friends pose on a fake boat at the amusement park at Coney Island in New York City.

Louis always thought about the meaning of the words to a song. "All songs display my life somewhat," he said. "You got to be thinking or feeling about something." He poured his feelings into his trumpet playing. His eyes closed. His cheeks puffed. Swaying with the music, he danced around the stage.

In 1930, Louis spent several months in California. There he met the popular singer and actor Bing Crosby. The two men became good friends.

By then, Louis and Lil had decided they couldn't live together anymore. Their marriage ended in divorce.

Bing Crosby sang many of the most popular songs of the 1930s.

Over the years, Louis's records had spread around the world. When Louis traveled to Europe, he found that people there loved his music. In Great Britain, he earned the nickname Satchmo, short for "Satchelmouth." (A satchel is a carrying case with a large opening.) "We should get friendly. I'm Satchmo," he told audiences.

In New York City, he appeared in a Broadway show called *Hot Chocolates*. One of its songs was "Ain't Misbehavin'." Louis helped make it a hit. Big bands with many musicians were popular in the 1930s. Louis often played solos with these bands.

This program shows that Louis played a solo before the second act of Hot Chocolates.

WEEK BEGINNING MONDAY EVENING, JULY 8, 1929
MATINEES THURSDAY AND SATURDAY

CONNIE'S
"HOT CHOCOLATES"
A New Tanskin Revel
WITH

PROGRAM CONTINUED

ENTRE'ACTE
Trumpet Solo by Louis Armstrong

ACT TWO

Scene 1
The Wedding of the Rabbit and the Bear

Hostess .... EDITH WILSON
Bunnies .... PAUL and THELMA MEERES
Bear .... BABY COX
Rabbit .... Madaline Belt
Fox .... Paul Bass
Monkeys .... Mary Prevall, Louise Williams, Natalie Long
Pussy-Cat .... Margaret Simms
Frogs .... Midnight Steppers
Sister Twister .... Louise Cook
Jackass .... Billy Maxey
Zebras .... Bon Bon Buddies
Birds .... Jubilee Singers

Scene 2
Harlem Street Scene
Billy Maxey, Dick Campbell, Frances Hubbard, Pearl Baines

PROGRAM CONTINUED ON NEXT PAGE

29

Louis brought his girlfriend, Alpha Smith (RIGHT), on his tour of Europe. The two were later married for a short time.

In 1932, Louis again went to Europe. In Copenhagen, Denmark, more than ten thousand people greeted him. They honored him with a flower bouquet shaped like a trumpet. But as the crowd's excitement grew, things got out of hand. People grabbed at Louis and tore off half his clothes.

Wherever he went, fans looked forward to his theme song, "When It's Sleepytime Down South." He sang about soft winds blowing, steamboats on the river, and dancing until dawn.

THE GREAT DEPRESSION

In the 1930s, the United States was suffering through the Great Depression. Millions of people lost their jobs, their homes, and their money. Louis felt sorry for those who had lost everything. At one concert in 1932, he learned that people nearby had no coal to warm their houses. So Louis ordered a ton of coal delivered to the theater. Everyone took some home.

The song reminded him of his childhood in New Orleans. His life wasn't at all like that anymore. Days seemed to fly by faster and faster. But Louis's special talent kept pushing him forward.

4 "BLUEBERRY HILL"

L ouis had not forgotten what it felt like to be poor. He lived a more comfortable life now. But helping others made him happy. So he always kept two rolls of cash in his pockets. One was for him to spend. From the other roll, he handed out money to needy people, friends, and fans.

In 1935, Louis began a long tour of the United States. Sometimes his band did shows in a different city each night. At age thirty-four, Louis once joked that he had spent "nine thousand hours" on buses and planes. But Louis knew he couldn't slow down if he wanted the band to do well.

Louis bows to the audience during a 1937 performance at the Paramount Theater in New York City. He always carried a white handkerchief onstage to wipe the sweat off his face.

World events soon changed the lives of all Americans. In December 1941, the United States entered World War II (1939–1945). Louis helped with the war effort at home. With his music, he entertained young soldiers at military bases.

Soldiers at Kelly Field air base in Texas show Louis how to fire a bazooka.

Louis met Lucille Wilson at the Cotton Club, a restaurant and theater in New York City. Louis's band played at the club, where Lucille was a dancer.

In 1942, Louis married Lucille Wilson. She was beautiful, loving, and smart. Like Louis's mother, Lucille also had good common sense. Louis told friends she was the perfect girl for him. They moved into a fine house in the Queens section of New York City. Their new home delighted Louis. He called the neighborhood kids "my little ice cream eaters."

That December, the couple spent their first Christmas together while on tour. In their hotel room, Lucille decorated a small Christmas tree. She carried it to every hotel they stayed in until New Year's Day.

Lucille drives while Louis plays a solo on a tour of Rome, Italy.

By this time, Louis was one of the most well-known Americans in the world. He had been the first African American to host a national radio show. He was also the first to star in a movie. In one film, he sang and played the trumpet for a nervous racehorse. In another, he played a tune for a dancing skeleton.

In the years after World War II, Louis and his new All Stars band traveled the country. They played in small towns and big cities. Some people said his music was old-fashioned. But huge crowds always came to listen.

In 1949, Louis recorded "Blueberry Hill." The song was about a man and a woman in love. The words told of the moon overhead and the wind blowing through the willows. This song wasn't jazz. It was country music. But it didn't matter. Audiences loved whatever Louis did.

In the 1950s, Louis worked harder than ever. He went on television and made more movies and records. He even wrote a book about his life. One magazine called Louis "the most important musical figure of all time."

LANGUAGE OF JAZZ

Louis made up slang words. *Chops* meant a musician's mouth and jaw or how well he played. *To jive* meant to play jazz. A *gutbucket* was a homemade string bass instrument. Louis called other musicians *Daddy* or *Pops*. They called him Pops too.

5 "WHAT A WONDERFUL WORLD"

"I never did want to be no big star, just always wanted to give a good show," Louis once said. "My life has been my music. It's always come first." Louis lived for the audience. He tried to please people the best way he knew—by singing and playing his horn.

In the 1950s, the U.S. government often sent Louis to other countries to spread goodwill. Many fans in the countries he visited spoke no English. But they understood his language—music. For African Americans, his success with people of all races made him a hero.

On June 23, 1959, the frantic pace of Louis's life caught up with him. He suffered a heart attack in Italy. He tried to slow down. But soon, his busy concert schedule continued. On May 22, 1963, he played for President John F. Kennedy.

In 1956, Louis recorded an album with another famous singer, Ella Fitzgerald (RIGHT).

Later in 1963, Louis recorded "Hello, Dolly!" Within months, it was the most popular song in the United States.

"I guess I've done 'Hello, Dolly!' about a million times," he said later. When he sang that song, he had fun with the audience. He puffed out his chest and made faces. He called this "jiving." And people loved it. On April 15, 1966, *Life* magazine put him on its cover. The writer of the story called him "America's Genius of Jazz."

Louis clowns around with the neighborhood kids on the steps of his home in Queens, New York, in the 1960s.

Louis and Lucille
visited the pyramids
of Egypt in the
1960s.

Over the next few
years, Louis's health got
worse. Doctors warned him that
playing the trumpet was bad for his heart.
So Louis sang more and played less. Still, he
had another heart attack. On July 6, 1971,
Louis Armstrong died. He was sixty-nine.

His wife Lucille received thousands of
sympathy cards. A funeral was held in a
small church in Queens, New York. The
place overflowed with people. Viewers in
sixteen countries watched the funeral on
television. The service ended with one of
Louis's best-loved songs: "When the Saints
Go Marching In."

Thousands of friends and fans came to Louis's funeral in Queens, New York.

A few days later, fifteen thousand fans turned out for another funeral in New Orleans. Musicians filled the air with the sounds of jazz. They marched proudly through the streets of New Orleans to honor their hometown hero.

Louis Armstrong's genius changed history. He helped make jazz one of the world's most popular kinds of music. Other musicians learned from his skills and his creativity. Trumpeter Miles Davis said, "You can't play anything on the horn that Louis hasn't played." Trumpeter Wynton Marsalis called Louis Armstrong's playing the "sound of America."

For almost fifty years, the Great Louis entertained millions of people as a singer, bandleader, movie star, and comedian. One of his many hit songs was "What a Wonderful World." In his deep, gravelly voice, he sang about the colors of the rainbow, friendship and love, and the hope that children bring. Louis Armstrong shared his warmth and his towering musical talent with the world. In his own special way, he made people everywhere feel wonderful.

SOME OF LOUIS ARMSTRONG'S HIT SONGS

"West End Blues"(1928)

"Ain't Misbehavin'" (1929)

"Stardust" (1931)

"When the Saints Go Marching In" (1938)

"Jeepers, Creepers" (1938)

"Blueberry Hill" (1949)

"Mack the Knife" (1955)

"Hello, Dolly!" (1964)

"What a Wonderful World" (1967)

TIMELINE

LOUIS ARMSTRONG
WAS BORN ON
AUGUST 4, 1901.

In the year . . .

1908   Louis entered school.   Age 7

1913   he was sent to Colored Waif's Home for Troubled Boys.   Age 11

1915   Louis supported his mother and sister with his horn playing.

1922   he joined King Oliver's Creole Jazz Band in Chicago, Illinois.   Age 21

1924   he married Lil Hardin and joined a New York City jazz band.

1925   he made the first of sixty-five recordings with his Hot Five band.   Age 24

1927   his mother, Mayann Armstrong, died.

1930   he performed in California.

1932   he played in Europe.
he appeared in a New York City musical, *Hot Chocolates*.   Age 31

1938   He was featured in the movie *Going Places* with Bing Crosby.

1941   the United States entered World War II. Louis played at U.S. military bases.

1942   he married Lucille Wilson.   Age 41

1954   he published *Louis Armstrong: Satchmo, My Life in New Orleans*.   Age 53

1956   he made an album with singer Ella Fitzgerald, *Ella and Louis*.

1964   "Hello, Dolly!" became the No. 1 song in United States.   Age 63

1971   he died on July 6.   Age 69

LOUIS ARMSTRONG AND RACISM

During his lifetime, Louis Armstrong often faced unfair treatment because he was an African American. In many places in the United States, separate drinking fountains and bathrooms were set up for black people and white people. Whites-only nightclubs had no bathrooms that black musicians could use. They had to go outside. Black band members could not stay in whites-only hotels. Sometimes Louis refused to perform at hotels where he couldn't stay overnight. During one of Louis's concerts in Tennessee, someone exploded dynamite outside. No one was hurt. But Louis knew how serious that could have been. He knew these things were not right. But laws and people's actions didn't change until Louis was in his sixties.

Yet through his music, he always reached out to people of all races. With warmth and love, he showed others respect, just as his mother had taught him. In this way, Louis spread goodwill and peace. Because of him, black musicians who came after him had more chances to succeed.

This 1950s Coca-Cola machine is marked for "White Customers Only!"

FURTHER READING

Ehrhardt, Karen. *This Jazz Man.* **New York: Harcourt Children's Books, 2006.** Find out about several other jazz musicians in this book filled with rhythm and rhymes.

Jones, Veda Boyd. *Jazz Age Poet: A Story about Langston Hughes.* **Minneapolis: Millbrook Press, 2006.** Learn about writer Langston Hughes, a popular figure in Harlem during Louis's years there.

McDonough, Yona Zeldis. *Who Was Louis Armstrong?* **New York: Grosset & Dunlap, 2004.** Read more about Louis's amazing career.

Pinkney, Andrea. *Duke Ellington: The Piano Prince and His Orchestra.* **New York: Hyperion, 2007.** Learn about another jazz legend of the 1900s, Duke Ellington.

WEBSITES

Jazz for Kids
http://www.pbs.org/jazz/biography/artist_id_armstrong_louis.htm
Explore the exciting world of jazz at this PBS website.

Satchmo.net: The Official Website of the Louis Armstrong House and Archives
http://www.satchmo.net
Hear Louis Armstrong play, read about his life, and see photos.

Smithsonian Jazz
http://www.smithsonianjazz.org/class/armstrong/la_class_1.asp Learn about jazz, read about jazz musicians, do activities, and find out more about Louis Armstrong.

Select Bibliography

Armstrong, Louis. *Satchmo: My Life in New Orleans.* Cambridge, MA: DaCapo Press, 1954.

Bergreen, Laurence. *Louis Armstrong: An Extravagant Life.* New York: Broadway Books, 1997.

Brothers, Thomas, ed. *Louis Armstrong: In His Own Words.* New York: Oxford University Press, 1999.

Giddins, Gary. *Satchmo: The Genius of Louis Armstrong.* Cambridge, MA: DaCapo Press, 1988.

Giddins, Gary. *Satchmo: Louis Armstrong, Master of American Music.* DVD. New York: Sony Music Entertainment and Multiprises, 1989, 2000.

Meckna, Michael. *Satchmo: The Louis Armstrong Encyclopedia.* Westport, CT: Greenwood Press, 2004.

Meryman, Richard. "An Interview with Louis Armstrong." *Life Magazine*, April 15, 1966.

Index

Acknowledgments

For photographs and artwork: © Hulton Archive/Getty Images, pp. 4, 19; © Duncan Schiedt, p. 7; © iStockphoto.com/Odelia Cohen, p. 8; AP Photo/Kenneth Lambert, p. 9; © Frank Driggs Collection/Hulton Archive/Getty Images, pp. 10, 13, 16, 17, 18, 22, 25, 30; © Bettmann/CORBIS, pp. 11, 41; Courtesy of the Louis Armstrong House Museum, Queens College, pp. 20, 21, 27, 29, 34, 35; AP Photo, p. 26; © John Kobal Foundation/Hulton Archive/Getty Images, p. 28; © Charles Peterson/Hulton Archive/Getty Images, p. 33; © Slim Aarons/Hulton Archive/Getty Images, p. 36; © Content Mine International/Alamy, p. 39; © POPPERFOTO/Alamy, p. 40; © Keystone/Getty Images, p. 42; Library of Congress, p. 45 (LC-USZ62-116815).

Front cover: © Lebrecht Music and Arts Photo Library/Alamy.
Back cover: AP Photo/Kenneth Lambert.

For quoted material: p. 11, Armstrong, Louis, *Satchmo: My Life in New Orleans,* (Cambridge, MA: DaCapo Press, 1954); pp. 13, 20, 27, 33, 40, Meryman, Richard, "An Interview with Louis Armstrong," *Life Magazine,* (April 15, 1966); pp. 13, 24-25, Giddins, Gary, *Satchmo: The Genius of Louis Armstrong,* (Cambridge, MA: DaCapo Press, 1988); p. 23, 37, Meckna, Michael, *Satchmo: The Louis Armstrong Encyclopedia,* (Westport, CT: Greenwood Press, 2004); p. 29, 35, 42 Giddins, Gary, *Satchmo: Louis Armstrong, Master of American Music,* DVD, New York: Sony Music Entertainment, Inc. and Multiprises, Inc., 1989, 2000); p. 38, 42, Burns, Ken, *The Definitive Louis Armstrong,* (New York: Sony Music Enterprises, 2000, jacket cover).